Not As Ugly

Poetry by

RANDY C. YOUNG

Not As Ugly

Poetry by

RANDY C. YOUNG

T&J PUBLISHERS

A SMALL INDEPENDENT PUBLISHER WITH A BIG VOICE

Printed in the United States of America by
T&J Publishers (Atlanta, GA.)
www.TandJPublishers.com

Cover Design by Timothy Flemming, Jr. (T&J Publishers)
Book Format/Layout by Timothy Flemming, Jr.

ISBN: 979-8-218-05287-4

To contact the author, go to:
Email: randyyoung@yahoo.com
Facebook: Randy Young

I dedicate this book to my parents Greta and Randy Moss, who always made me believe I can do whatever I want.

"Dwell on the beauty of life. Watch the stars,
and see yourself running with them."
—Marcus Aurelius

Table of Contents

When

When you can get burned
 and wear the scar like a patch
When you can let pressure pound
 and not worry about the match
When you can keep your head up
 while the only way is down
When you can listen even when
 your hearing is not surround sound
When you can welcome death,
 but try your hardest to live
When you can have nearly nothing,
 but still willing to give
When you can accept help when
 it's the last thing you want
When you can do what's best for you
 while others point and taunt
When you can lose a lifeline
 just so you can live
When you can hold on
 when it's up you want to give
When you can find a way where
 there doesn't seem like any
When you can keep going
 even though you don't have plenty
When you can ingest a tube
 through what make you man
When you can survive,
 even though you were hit when you ran
When you can lose it all
 and get back double

You will see why
 I am not afraid of trouble

A Touch Of Sound

Breaking barriers, with a touch of the fingertip
Staying in grace, while biting myself on the lip
Nervous, no, a habit picked up as a game on court
Athletic, maybe, but thing wasn't playing a sport
Change did come, let's listen to here and now
A Touch of Sound, never knew when, where, how
Pouring until love overflow into the river and spread
Merciful thoughts seem to be barred inside head
Showing soul bearing fruit of labor day, ready set
A pilot of emotions that steers cautiously in jet

Waiting On Time

Time I'm waiting on, I'm waiting on time
Staying ready, reaction at the drop of a dime
Through the mechanics showing prosperity
See through, notice the perfect clarity

Clear conscience, waiting to see the moon
Darkness ascends, now waiting daylight soon
Waiting, be patient, there are bonds to make
Staring through glass, concentration break
Waiting on a time where I am there to wallow
Suck it up, now my pride I have to swallow
Wait on me, but the weight a tad bit over
Good luck here, my little four leaf clover

Kissed By Fire

A slight touch that led to happiness for a lifetime
Pain unbearable, cried out in the sense of a mime
Veil over eyes, vision is blurred nothing is clear
Would go off on what was told, but it's hard to hear
No not average, greatness pumps through veins
Aching, let's lay in the bed while it's cold and rains
Rain puts out the fire, that burning sensation fed
Mindset to do wrong, fighting with personnel led
Mentality of saint, but actions may be deceived
A true battle between good and Evil which is believed
From the fire that kissed a Young boy, a stain remain
Close calls and good decisions, intuition to gain
Framework to a better life, the day has yet begun
Stand still and tall even though height says run
Managing to deliberate then penetrate the mind
With thought throughout the nerves, teeth grind
Same fire that kissed that Young boy built man
Kiss gave that Young boy a spark to be all he can

Patiently Waiting

A tie in time, may as well wait
To walk without sight is a test of fate
Emotions overwhelm as full as a lake
Do what's right for goodness sake
Others are viewed, we automatically rate
We are only human, there's nothing to hate
Noticing another is sweet as cake
Inner thoughts heat, then bake
A guiding light approaching from rear
Must enjoy everyday that one is here
Day will come, back against the wall
Must remember what comes over all
Full speed ahead, without shedding a tear
Eyebrows down, no matter what's the fear
Feeling down, there's someone to call
This world is a battle of wits, so brawl
The moment is now, and we are at war
Gripping pen until hand is sore
It's a show, let everyone look
Sacrifice the pawn to save the rook
Battle from heart to strengthen core
Giving all, but asking for more
Searching for a care, every cranny and nook
Sorry all out, something others took

Looking Forward

People, places, and things conquer the mind
Moving forward at a pace, but still left behind
Judgment passed, comparison made about the next
Stop and think, before taking it out of original context
Not valuable can be replaced in a whisk
Especially outdated, see the toss of disk
Now rewarded for crimes and pillage
To raise children it takes a village
Remembering what one will soon forget
Crime and punishment, does the sentence fit
A fuse of faith waiting to ignite
Having ambition high as a kite
The difference is tried and true
Done by many, accomplished by few

Clock Work

A place known for its currency exchange
So selling for profit is not at all strange
It's all about a number, more digits to figure
Pondering throughout the day to get richer
Meditating often, listening to music, dance
Awaiting on turns, patience until it's chance
Listening and looking for a number called
From full head of hair, to gray, skipping bald
Wake up, work everyday from nine to five
Hustling past struggle know how to survive
College is a great way to further education
Hoping to be hired at a high pay occupation
Being born rich has to be as good as it gets
Worried about how many ways it splits
The amount paid gets judged by time
And when you leave, you can't take a dime

Good And Evil

The devil look up to me while I look up to God
To see the world through another's eyes are odd
When there's no up, looking to the devil for answers
The devil ignores the question, while giving cancers
God doesn't come when wanted, but in need
To listen to the devil, it's God I want I plead
God listens to me as well as he talks
The devil often runs, while God walks
God continues to bless and I let it be
The devil destroys everything he see
The devil hates, while God shares his love
The devil is below, God triumphs above
They are as different as fire and ice
Away with the devil, take God's advice

This Little Life Of Mine

Thinking big, living a life far from mediocre
Enjoying life, you would think I'm drunk when sober
High off life, everyday natural state of mentality
Convinced that this is greatness and not a fallacy
Shining as far as the twinkle in my eye goes
Satisfying, as in breakfast smells hitting nose
Up early, not wasting time on mere daydreaming
Putting in action, my dreams, goals together seeming
Splish splash of water as it hit the dishes
Always cautious, so I mean all my wishes
Dreams come true, living them not hard at all
The highway to easy street detour to mall
Booking daily, I really love my new gig
This little life of mine may seem little to you, but to me it's big

Vision Of The Future

Brighter than a droplet of water by the sun's light
Airborne through a nature, but similar to flight
Exceeding expectations to failure, seem blind
With a heart on the sleeve, seeping everything kind
Wishful thinking, a future filled with greatness
A planner, goal orientated, do away pessimist

In A State Of Being

Replenish handling situations well and go far
Seeking the justice that is withstood by bar
Hurdling over obstacles meant to stop
A long way from home in mind set prop
Mistaking courage for some type of guilt
Reinacting life from before the time spilt
Encouraging rememberance of a new day
Twisting minds in an entirely new way

In The Making

With a sense of confidence all in the making
Going from place to place without breaking
Nonchalant fatigue still visible enough
In and out staying there after it's tough
Managing dialogue even when shutout
Realizing speaking means less to shout
Glamour is less when equipped without seeing
Time becomes less when living is without being

Living In The Past

The anniversary of an action that breathes life
A moment in time that seemed to be strife
Grew into a lesson well learned and carried on
A night like this where must all see the sun
Few past events make a way thats unbearable
By the side on in a way that can become comparable
A sign that's clear underway an legible
Competing in life, now that's not measurable

In Love With Life

As day turns to night, I enjoy them both
In Love with Life, my new solemn oath
What joy life brings, here as far as there
I travel life's roads, without a worry or care
Lessen all drama, bring peace and tranquility
Life's newborn, what an idealistic delivery
Incubator not needed, breathing just fine
Oh how I'm in love with this little life of mine

Two Hearts, One Beat

Two Hearts, One Beat, together a life we share
How I find a great comfort, knowing you are there
Two Hearts, One Beat, we travel many roads
How I find joy, knowing you help carry loads
Two Hearts, One Beat, we are in sync like a watch
How I am satisfied, knowing it's not just any notch
Two Hearts, One Beat, wouldn't have it another way
How I find pleasure in your smile, not letting it astray

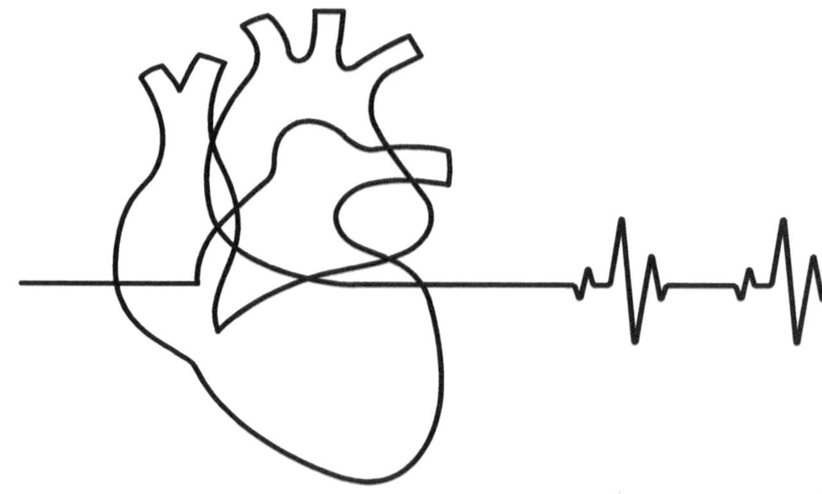

Curing Fear

For things that surpass a count to measure
Give in to desires that bring about pleasure
No matter the feat or the amount to destination
Go and conquer be king of that current equation
A try and fail is merely a lesson that was learned
Look forward, but remember the try and fail earned
Life comes with obstacles that are a subsequent distraction
Live your life to the fullest just to see what will happen

Proud

Proud of what I have and the things I do
Proud to have the people in my life, many or few
Proud of what I've done over the years I've grown
Proud of who I've met, ones that's here and gone
Proud of what I can do because of my health
I'm just proud of me, yes I'm proud of myself

Out And About

Wind in my hair as I stare ahead
Mild caution as I tie my dread
Phone in use as I talk that talk
Stern never stumbling since I could walk
Standing tall, but height wasn't given to me
Use it as a weapon, I would rather pee
To see me growing it's love's newfound
Squatting, head high and feet off of ground
Function normal, but that's overrated
To love oneself is no means to be hated
Film rolls a life close to a movie
Favors done, but after watch how you do me

Reasons

A reason in which one saves the matter
Monetary differences implementing a ladder
Climbing to the top no matter the height
Still above water even if that causes plight
After withstanding reasons meant to sink
Capturing all beauties ending with a blink
Eyes gaze as the nerves remove shaking
Year after year reasons are in the making
No matter friend, sister, or a brother
Your reasons are not to satisfy another

Silent Cries

Can you hear the silent cries? The ones that creep at night
The silent cries, the silent cries that bark less than bite
Can you hear them? What a soothing sound they make
From the silent cries, they make you weak and then shake
Lured into a makeshift trap like a rat after the cheddar cheese
Silent cries that you have no other choice than drop to knees
Staying bowed even though you want the decision to rise
Tears so thick that you imagine it's blood coming from eyes
Can you hear the silent cries? Because they are the loudest
Imagine living in a world where you don't need acknowledgment
to be proudest

Since The Beginning Of Time

Thorough investigation of the hesitation that caused devastation
A place for you, a place for me, a place for we I'm making
Livable, forgivable, my hands are restricted, tied, own
Message the messenger, delete the prototype from phone
Believable, deceivable giving a reason for the reasonable
Price is right, the time is now, adding flavor to what's seasonable
Days pass, months last, been that way since the beginning of time
Just a thought, I'm what the lions brought, guess you can say I'm
in my mind

Change

Thank God there have been some changes that we knew in the past
For the ones who stood up so that the past wouldn't last
From being restricted, and of shackles and a chain
Being abused physically and as well as the brain
"A change will come" they shouted as they march
Some freedoms were manifested and that's a good part
A change in direction and appearance, not of the heart
Through change we accomplish, but stlll in need of a fresh start

Strangers

Affiliating an affiliation with an affiliate that is not yet known
Living where the rule is that we must have something to own
Making moves with the move to make a pipe withstand pressure
On all fours a dog's life where it started I can not measure
With a wish in mind and a heart to match like the drugs passed
Through an image away with images live and let it be gassed

Loud Silence

Lost care fed through the tube of life
excreting passion for pain
Maintaining excellence while eating my words
that drip like rain
Wet from excitement that deals with a cure
that expells what to endure
Strength weakening for that to the basics is learned,
but far from pure
White lies change the efficiency of what's said
to assure the trust
Devastating to manage though a thorough
solution is now a must
Aging age with an age that carries wisdom
and knowledge of surgery
Went through a transition of transaction
with nothing short of emergency

A Life To Live

I have a life to live following the tears I've shed
Pain and degradation knowing my soul has bled
A true calling of the strife from endurance I survive
I channel my anger, control my energy count back from five
influence the influencer a debate of great nature
But still left empty not knowing what fills this crater
To live on and live strong with knowledge and reason
I have a life to live even though it changes like the season

Pain

Going or coming, a moment to come in history
Facing a reaper that's grim and to talk about misery
In company of many, fighting for what is now good
Dodging the man taking lives, pull down his hood
Managing to stay free for now, later not determined
Feel fire burning soul, now with her on arm squirmed
He lies near her with her in a distance three protect
Now The Pan is near home, but showing respect
In the air it lives, not knowing when The Pan leaving
Constant lives shattering, ready to be done grieving

Forbidden Fruit

Your eyes looked through my soul in a way that defined me
I stared a the gaze from up close thinking this can not be
A wonder of amaze viewed as all out in a ransom of words
Proper precaution taken with the words started to be slurred
My baby my baby left outside to be a frozen statue of what was
Maintaining to be absent in presence to of a recognition of a buzz

Your Allure

With dark eyes surrounded by a chocolate exterior
Your sexiness I watch as if I'm staring in a mirror
Hair so unique of a style that I always bat an eye
Smile hidden, the mystery you show well enough to sigh
Willing to show you how hard things are in my era
A generational curse, my, a rise for you, thanks Sarah
I can tell of your smile as you follow with a giggle
Rather a true statement than to imagine your booty jiggle

Degraded Pain

Up at two a. m., at two a. m. I'm up
Fighting for my food, the runt form of a pup
Breast fed no day, but I am not going hungry
Teammates never, highly spoken in my lonely
This pain is degraded, I have degraded pain
Not an ache on me yet, I get sleepy in the rain
Facing truth and optimism, nothing I didn't know
Searching for new endeavors, can you tell me where to go?
Gas breeds fire, eyes heavy, but palms are itching
Heart speeds up, so I know the superstition
I have dirty nails it is dirty nails I have
Counting up daily, I get stingy with my math
Degraded Pain this is, this pain is degraded
All I asked for, so I ask why hate it?

My Inspiration

You are my inspiration, you are my heart
You and me were meant from the start
You are my love, you are my everything
The love you have makes my heart sing
To the heavens and below for you I go
I love you, I just thought you should know

With You

Our love stands tall, ready for what is brought
I threw my heart, and waited for it to be caught
You were there, with open hand, knowing it's fragile
My heart didn't break, being with you has it agile
Holding you close, feeling the beat causes butterflies
Enticed by your warmth, I see love through your eyes

Love

You plus me equals love
We soar high as a dove
Over mountains we leap sow
Into closed arms we reap
Sow into a brief kiss
My Misses never Miss
I will love you for life
Happy I made you my wife

You Have A Good Heart

Pounding to love, care, and notice
In life can sometimes lose focus
You set your sight on what to achieve
PUtting time into it now start to believe
In you, there is a light that must shine
From a place deeper than stars align
In a world where there are outcasts
Your inner glow is the memory that lasts
Throughout the days, and brighten nights
A strength ones who fought now plights
Suggest to be an everlasting greed
To see prosperity and everyone succeed

Short And Sweet

In a daze, thoughtful ways, how to caress your skin
Imagine, cotton soft, with memories cause grin
Between us, between you, dreaming moments of bliss
Darkened night, but with joy, sharing of a first kiss
Lips emerge, the thought sit, surely withstood pleasure
All over, from slight touch, could be new endeavor
Set sights, merge now, must now part the way
For now, sun shining, the beauty is in day
Never end, something great, found the day that met night
Full moon, perfection, that is a perfect sight
Brown eyes, heavenly, a lust for the dark
Intertwined, images, hoisted legs hitting mark
Up and down, back and forth, time out for reason
Well known, in lust, giving in now certain

Mom

Your smile shines, I the son, and the daughter of life
A brother, from Mom, never words of a knife
You carried, all of us, in a loving embrace
Did it all, with the dimples, always showing on face
Energetic, radiant, nothing but love you seep
Positive, and humble, showing not to be weak
Strength excelled, a way made, never not felt your love
Heaven sent, gift of life, great as the stars above
Looking up, change has come, you have taught us so much
Love is Mom, Mom is love, reaching out to grasp such

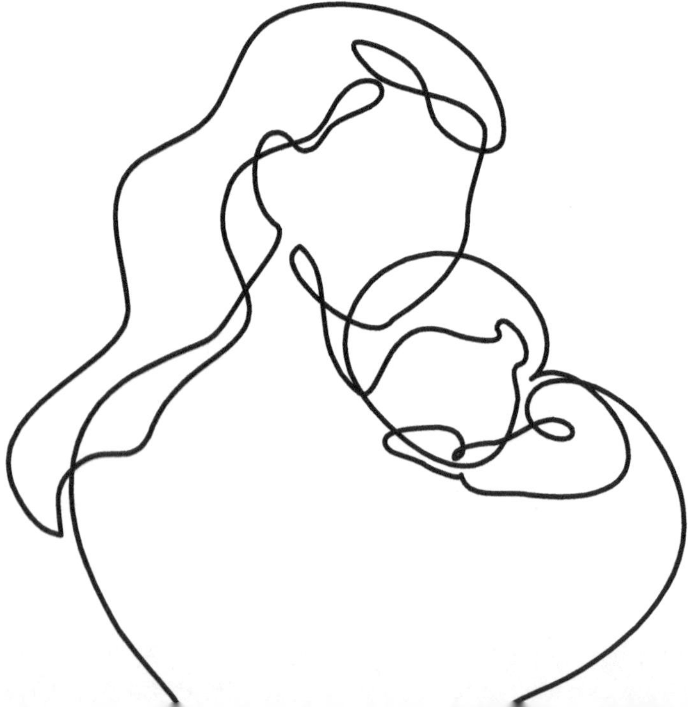

Bittersweet

The phone rang, I answered, not knowing who's online
A phone call, changed my life, memory of being supine
When I woke, a deep breath, along with a pipes tug
From within, still fighting, woken with parents hug
In so tight, depleted, my strength was there no more
Loving thoughts, this was two, being rolled through the door
Slid open, face to roof, forward to next venue
Lights were bright, sights were set, pipe by neck when I chew
Not Mom's food, side by side, she leaned as I rocked
Strength pouring, still fighting, off my feet I was knocked
Door opened, blown away, seeing my belly cut open
All is well, I am great, dreaming with eyes open

Me And You

Eye to eye, hand on thigh, destination achieved
Climactic, through convo, me not easily believed
Circumstance, alone time, you decide what we do
Whatever, I am down, live among the proud few
Are like me, not alone, though seen as a rare breed
Seldom seen, I am ready, your body I can read
Allowed me, you allow, a session for us both
Me and you, you and me, together for new growth

My Sunshine

Here we are, time to be, with all light shining in
My heart beats, double time, satisfied with your grin
Pearly whites, ear to ear, my teachings to be humble
Love to have, just don't brag, keep it silent don't stumble
Trouble comes, please be wise, wisdom comes before age
Time in life, my heart swells, what's a book with no page

Control

Stay in it, day by day, control actions and words
Say what's meant, do what's needed, control all of your thoughts
Positive, they make sense, control your fear all times
Morning to night, day to dark, control tone forever
Express mind, do not yell, control emotions correct
Make them right, do not cover, we must learn to control
Tendencies, and habits, we must learn to control

Up And Up

Up and up, where we go, now away with troubles
Nonetheless, make it through, now having joy doubles
Not problems, no mischief, for today will be great
We are now, wilful change, a sacrifice of rate
Worth the wait, proved worthy, finish what was began
Remember, what was done, keepsake for inner ran
Left in blur, let light shine, glowing off sun's rays
Light shines bright, on in dark, goodness shines throughout days

Eyes Open

Open your eyes, you can learn a lesson
If so, you can be done with stressing
No more stressing, you can start to bloom
Open to all, you can enjoy your room
A clean space can stop all depression
Will now see the food in every session

Broken Spanish

I speak like no mind of me to hear
Walking in a path that surpass fear
Igniting a being that deepens in breed
Knowing I contain necessities of seed
Spill of overwhelming pressure, timeout
A game that must be played with shout
Loudness in the silence, prefer sound
Of the action of maintaining ground
Feet down, now a grasp on reality
For I am the entity through casualty

Beautiful

Insides stretch, widening, after a look showed pass
Entangled, intertwined, motions a success as I grasp
I grasp you, you grasp air, our bodies begin to get moist
I'm on you, you're on nine, in the air your legs are hoist
Passion screams, voices go, can hear a high from your breathing
In and out, back and forth, to me your climax is achieving.

Side By Side

Side by side, hand in hand, steps taken in life together
With you, on my mind, no storm I can not weather
Sun shining, beautiful, triumph whelms through my breathing
In and out, back and forth, picture of our love exceeding
High mountains, low waters, throughout
the globe and surroundings
Watch closely, taking steps, closer to new great arousings
Hard as steel, entrance met, may be irregular
Membrane throbs, bodies shake, the bed frame we alter,
But instead, side by side, I let you choose the way
Left or right, up or down, as long as it's with you I lay.

Fear Wrath

Close to the flesh an obvious touch
Finished beginnings seemed too much
Seen to be a cordial invitation
Prolonged looks insight the hesitation
Would've been the perfect picture, but missing a piece
Such beautiful creatures, but after all they are a lease
Spring chickens even age with time
Cute smiles, drinks with lime
With a walk like that feel the stares
Searching for a duplicate, but no one pairs
Found to be a blessing like in sternutation
Doing everything in your name no matter the situation
Delete chances WHILE GOING ON TO BE SURE
Questioning words coming from a place so pure
Rise for the occasion never to fall
Waiting on arrival beckoning at every call
In a grasp never to reach out
Storm before weather expect a clout
Repel the trust as an inoculation

Anew Vision

To come out of the blue while remaining to stay visible
A new ambiance in life while condition is critical
While life is new, still impulses of fear
Listening to them rejoice, a better day is near
A bridge of trouble, not knowing where to cross
A crumpet of faith and belief with a mere toss
Blood shed, sweat shed, even a tear
Stay complacent. Goals will not veer
Nothing is eaten with the fork in the road
Feet up and off goes the load
Balance is kept, only through peace
The body given is only a lease
Time spent is promised by no on adieu
Good or bad, when it's over it's through
Moment has come to anew the vision
Focused excelling on precision

In A Time The World Is Ruled By The Internet

In a time the world is ruled by internet browser
One can find out a person's life by a device in their trouser
Opinions are broadcast as a fact
Crucifying another for the way they act
Arguments start of another's thought
Sneaky person pray not to get caught
Video posted of an act related to violence
Relationships suffer from lack of silence
In a time the world is ruled by internet browser
One can find out a person's life by a device in their trouser
Take heed to the icon marked privacy
Nothing is copyrighted free to piracy
Be mindful that the nudity is superficial
Marked not by name, but an initial
There is good also, depending on the request
An invitation to accept, declining the rest
In a time the world is ruled by internet browser
One can find out a person's life by a device in their trouser
Search with knowledge of picking out a scam
Devices off, due to an exam
The knowledge of gossip out to broaden horizon
No matter the carrier T-Mobile, Sprint, or Verizon
Treating an opinion as if it were the truth
Envying the personnel that used the phone booth
In a time the world is ruled by internet browser
One can find out a person's life by a device in their trouser

What To Do

Words fall to the page
Been called bitter, causes rage
Seen calm, seemingly different
Anger builds, steady persistent
Like ocean waves, rise
Stare blankly at demise
Build and tower until crash
Before crash a voice speaks
Listening ears, eyes leaks
Survivors guilt causes a tremor
The clear path becoming dimmer
Another stare searching for reason
Lesser grounds called treason
Yet a promise to contradict
Leads to unclear choice picked

Wonderful Night

Pleasantness is quite infectious
Come to a smile to detect us
A sight to see one presume
Faint from the aroma of sweet perfume
Enlightened in a land of bliss
Never to end a night like this
Stars out accompanied by a full moon
Thankful for what's now knowing it ends soon
Cordial invitation approach and bow
Movement over later than now
Having an experience one would wish, so cherish
Whisked away, it's only the breath that perish
A night like this found, so beautiful
Gaze into each others eyes, feelings mutual
A moment in time one can only dream
Discovered by us, now feeling supreme

Sayings

To be accepted by all is to be loved by none
Judged and mocked by more than a few
A trait in us all, the pleasing has only begun
On trial, evidence pointing, want to start anew
Some would rather be judged by twelve than carried by six
Everyone is entitled to one's own choice
To assure a consequence is not a bag of tricks
Laws are enforced and given a voice
The pot calling the kettle black
In a sense, we are the same
Criticizing for what others lack
Problems arise with or without fame
If it weren't for bad luck there wouldn't be any luck at all
One is not put in what they can't handle
Walk by faith, not by sight, especially if one fall
If done so it's the obstacle that will dismantle

Small World After All

Visiting a land of bliss
Right ahead, can not miss
Better place, better view
May miss morning dew
Land for places wide
Once chained, free inside
Nothing said, quiet to keep
Not a sound, not a peep
Once there, now gone
Getting out comfort zone
What's new, get silly
Trade in money, really
Paid off, no debt
Moving on, no regret
Making all short and sweet
New attitude, now elite
Sacrifice bone and skin
Not to need again

Winners

Don't lose head, the brain it contain
It's a movement, but still must remain
By one self is considered to be lonely
Loving the woman, as if she is the world's only
Guide accompanied by a light
A journey to come, despite plight
Therefore it's a land of wonder
Living on top, afterwards go under
Scents are therapeutic, let them work
Wildlife is tamed, but scenery is berserk
Speak into existence, dream an appearance
Open the heart, make a clearance
Put in, overcome, keep in drive
Follow the dream, one can thrive
Figure out what to do until it's done
Finish back burners until all is won

Future Goals

Hanging at the end of the rope
Life's not a deal, but find ways to cope
Safety is an issue to consider before proceeding
When there is talent, the best is exceeding
Find a measurement of progress
Reduce whatever causes stress
Make sure achievements are monumental
Anything short of detrimental
Dive right in with all necessary tools
A jungle out there, sharks in pools
Search jobs wide and specific
Real life, anything, but hieroglyphic
A new ambiance of pain
Aimed for an emotional gain
Truth comes to the next being
Nothing more honest than the eyes seeing
A way to make the next move
Don't leave anything else to prove

Just A Thought

Getting bruises from sound, as if it were a weapon
Running water over the body, as if it were protection
In same situation, looking for change
Similar circumstance expecting different results, deranged
No refreshments thank you, just fuel to the flame
Going back to retry, as if it were a game
No excuses please, just misunderstanding
After speech it is still demanding
Thoughts concur after words hesitate
Now its mind one will infiltrate
Water spills, burning a hole in the surface
Stagnant, there goes one more purchase
Going through extreme measure for peace
After all, life is only a lease
A lived life is a success
Visualized death is a guess

New Heights

Soaring to new heights without a touch
Being a man, there are problems to confront
Individuals in face with advice of much
Swings from the strongest become a bunt
Going nowhere fast despite strive
Fearing a shadow that hasn't been seen
Wonder the meaning being alive
Bypassing mercy, the idea of torture is keen
At the moment that sweat transpire
A thought of worry entered the head
On a mission to acquire
From moment awake, until time for bed
Great, life turning a blind eye
A stand still, awaiting opportunity
Releasing at the end a deep sigh
To leave without abandoning community

Bitter Sweet

The ugly truth heard from the beautiful lies told
The essence of youth remembered by days of getting old
Blessings bestowed upon those who are in need
Do not disregard, but take heed to his creed
In a threat to exemplify, greed marks a lot
Penny pinching everyday until the corpse rot
Filling holes with this and that keeping stomach off empty
Nervous minded in hearing so when talked to, say gently
Rock sideways, looking out the window to get a better view
Seeing how it is to be appreciated for nothing that you do
Recall a simpler time from heaven's whisper
From the thought of going on, eyes glitter
Strength comes from the obstacles faced
Further gone, weaknesses are replaced
Dealing with adversity, must keep focus
Far off, or near by, must find locus
Day by day struggle managing, dealing
To see what is to become, that part revealing

The Troll

In a land of make believe a higher power prevail
Dungeons and dragons, a pirate ship sets sail
Found the way to a troll with an issue
Wipes snot from nose, without a tissue
Seem solid at periods, yet others the colors vague
Pills, potions, and tricks attempting to start a plague
Lured in by magnificent contraptions
Promising to encounter all satisfactions
Pursue at will, don't be fooled by charm
With spiky hair, mustache, and hair overflowing from arm
The troll is not a dummy, that must be clear
Insecurities are hidden by being immovable by fear
The troll becomes larger in voice to hide size
Rival being pigheaded, make pressures to rise
Night comes a measure to scheme and plot
Jealousy embeds the troll, wanting what I got
The troll can't see that he's everyone's envy
Now he lives days on and with the witches curse that's plenty

Advice

Bursting out of the shoes, once said too big
Falling in the same grave one had to dig
Stick to the movements, being sure they are precise
Focus over all, let whatever follows be suffice
Notice everything, stay trained in the art
Must take mental pictures before the start
Give small gifts, make sure to balance
Keep closed eyes, forgiving others talents
Know weakness. Keeping strengths to illuminate
Keep calm head when others imitate
Trust who is to be trusted, one may push in
Make statements true or false, lesson taught to begin
A steady heart, steadier mind, goes a long way
Having a place to sleep during night, eat in day
Practice and professionalize speech
Learn to own is each

Fear

Seeing death around the corner, pigtails and beads
Hard to get a blood pressure because the heart stampedes
Caught peaking, waiting on a fall
Condemned onset for life's brawl
Found behind safe, surrounded with bars
Quickly mind drifts, the vision of piling cars
One shot, right place, sent below earth
Gift of life ended, presentation of stillbirth
Screams from a mother pacing the floor
Excitement caused to faint, opening the door
Goodbyes are said, moment to preempt
Feeling of drowning above water, let's exempt
Intentions are pure, do not misconstrue
Who's eye comes first, a question of few
Dream of the day when no longer can hear
Ask the question, what is fear

Love And Happiness

Love for sale any takers
Omitting all the heartbreakers
Looking into the future as just another date
Covering trail with truth often leave lies to fabricate
Looking at watch said to come soon
Left this morning, my dear it's now noon
Tired of being tired, left with much grief
Awaiting the right time, acquaintance more than brief
In the eyes of another nothing to furlong
Arguementive about what is had so strong
Love you, Love you not, the petal pushed to the floor
Future plans, anal thoughts of the woman one adore
Careful with love when there's a creeping thought of hate
Wishing never met while adhering to a clean slate
Fuel and passion burns deep remember to refuel
The makings of being special and true used for tool

All About Money

Money comes money goes, some more than others
Ways to get money, ways to spend money, idea hovers
A piece of paper valued by marks
If any is taken a conflict that sparks
Aquiring new things without any purpose
Bells, whistles, and rings walking around nervous
Places to go, people to see, that's the movement
How to act, a way to be, what's the improvement
Opinions are gathered by who scheme
Fear of accomplishment stay in between
Not enough money marks stress
Too much money not enough kindness
Building ego off what can be bought
Often forgetting the lesson that's taught
From making to spending money goes in money comes out
Do what you will with the money, but afterwards don't pout

Shut Up And Listen

Shut up and listen
Skin shine eyes glisten
Be quiet open your ears
Pulled on, thoughts or fears
Brushed back silent wave
Dig within now pave
Pushed away now refresh
Wish was longer covered in mesh
Brushed followed swing
Scratched down a focal thing
Focused on and played with
Knowing existence so no myth
Attention goes to lowest of the back
Future thoughts of what on now lack
Rubbed over now lift
Either way a gift

Legit Movement

The way moved is a happenstance
Turns head the paper dance
Blows breath wonder smell
Belch stinks hard to tell
Deepened thoughts stomps lurk
Pops neck some jerk
Feet ready body resign
Words fall to lay body supine
Strange world nose scratched
Decision made plan hatched
Looking forward to a better tomorrow
Leave behind the pain and sorrow
Hand on knee difference search
Bird on a limb obvious perch
Lean forward view of the word
Less than nothing that's absurd

Managing Anger

Temper flare stomach boiling
Sight blurry Inners coiling
Teeth grit breath exhaled
Feeling of pillage thought impaled
Looks down head pounds
Visions lurk of last rounds
Scratches head looks away
Inhales deeply saw stay
Rolls eyes presses back
Does again for what didn't lack
Tip of tongue bridge of nose
Eyes closed praying pose
Forehead wiped picks up pen
Deep sorrow before exhaling again
Begging for power wishing for strength
Looks back to hair staying for length
Sky falls tons of confusion
Life lies caught in illusion
Doubt standards picks up stress
Scratch head a wonderful mess

The Race

Light shines here and yonder
Hands up to keep sun from face
A timid fidget then ponder
One from behind has picked up pace
Tough skin cut victory will bleed
Caused by the sharpness of a feather
Said enough now take heed
Occasion is suffice given this beautiful weather
Temperature just right, wind blow mild
Sun beaming less enough not to sweat
Shortness of breath, oxygen tender and wild
Imaging having the engine of a jet
Ornery position a win if any
Putting in one step at a time
Started with wishes, this was a gimmie
A win but finishes like slime

Incomplete

Work daily a slave of money
Often on the spot like Johnny
To glory be the recipient
Lights glow they seem ambient
At the end one must pick
Decision to be made long or quick
Hands out worry of only two
Others follow when one is through
Looking towards the past then it dawns
Think more than single moves use pawns
Over time one will awaken
Soft as a pillow pain taken
Away with kind words let speak
Finding out this is no place for the weak
Knowing all have own trials
But different action, different styles
Everyone is not basic, all are unique
Sights set out on whatever one seek

Follower

Never lead follow the fleet
To the days of not giving up a seat
Close eyes follow the dream
Single player never used a team
No direction follow the road
Welcome to a humble abode
Health choice follow the strong
Feeling like this isn't a place to belong
Done with lies follow the truth
Hard to overcome followed as youth
Leave weak follow with pride
Doing that dead inside
Slow women follow the man
Try and try with all one can
Try no more follow the doer
Tired of leading a life of manure
Time has come to follow and plead
How can one follow when destiny is to lead
Now that's done follow to sate
All the following one hasn't ate
At the beginning follow the end
Hard to follow on bended knees friend
Know to follow, follow the heart
Within the body, follow to start
Follow the heart, must follow the mind
There are leaders and followers throughout mankind

The Struggle Is Real

Cold from lack of heat
Cautious, hole in seat
Worried about what to eat
Game of life can't be beat
Heating water to take a bath
Wondering is this God's wrath
Minimizing activities after school
Are these blessings to a fool
Could wash didn't have enough to dry
Learning how to live without a tear from the eye
Strong survive, chosen few
In debt to maintain
Everyday in pain
Open heart only to be mocked
Fighter aboard should've been socked
Bed arrangements weren't ideal
Boy, girl, this can't be real

What Does Love Mean To You?

Love is what love does
Forget what was
Obscure thoughts wondering from below or above
To give up the challenge who needs love
Everyone questions in the face of adversity
Found in everyday living or university
There isn't a drug that measures
Being guilty of unspoken pleasures
Between the two, one strong bond
This magic consists of no wand
Living without is no longer thought
Staring at the beauty not worried about getting caught
Love is knowing the next move
Often, but not always in the groove
Some adhere to opportunity, some wait
No matter the choice love is great
Drastic measures come to please
Mistakes happen, drop to knees
Two may become three, maybe four or more
To some it doesn't matter what comes adore
Feeling like a winner with that person
No matter what is said during arguing cursing

Daddy Long Stroke

Lesson learned on probability
State the change alternating stability
New sense after persuasion
Pheromone chaser every occasion
Deepened sound soultry soul
Pick up then roll
Given choices out of suggestions
Same here multiple erections
Must decide love or lust
Playing a position stay must
Find ways to make melt
Ready at the snap of a belt
Pictured in the form of butter
Drip, drop, the panties flutter
Lined up where I'm going
Daddy Long Stroke you not knowing

Autumn

Sky is dim, leaves topple
Games played, balls bobble
Daily awaiting the suns image
Looking above counting linage
After awaking to a ground of mush
Damp twigs of what was a bush
What was hot is now a slight chill
Due to circumstance shopping centers cut a deal
Prices paid clothes bought
Future training merely thought
Thinking back change is near
Howling winds it is hear
Dull skies, sad area
No more hysteria
Cheap thanks to a sale
Reason why never can tell
Gas prices on the floor
Filling up at every store

Sun's Out

A breeze blows, trees swing from side to side
Rocks thrown across the water skip, then glide
Children play excited, running behind the pet
Utilizing sprinklers just to get wet
Outside games are an option in favor
Competition followed by a friendly wager
Great time to break for a bottle of water
Or a cherry icee for only a quarter
If attitude come from any buffone
Retaliate by tossing a water balloon
Fun and games cause joy and laughter
The time is now. Not concerned with after

World's Strongest Man

Trees uproot from an exhale
Missions of life now stale
Miracles pulled off left a state of confusion
No one is greater, truth or illusion
Overcoming restraints with such raw aggression
Once staring down the barrel, now in that profession
Less than a fog, somewhat in a mist
Progression is made by the bens of a wrist
Twists, turns, really doesn't matter
Grounds shake from the feel of a patter
Rocks crumble in the palm of the hand
Discentigraited, rolling from the flesh like sand
Worry not from what one see
Do not frown, beg, nor plea
Shots were taken by circumstance
Much needed in order to advance
Trials and tribulations come with travel
Strong, yet a heart of gravel

Growing Up

Problems are hidden to make sure innocence is preserved
Dealing with the consequence of not telling
the reason time served
Time ticks seconds, minutes, hours, then days
Months to years seen stuck in ways
Tell not how to behave
Discard lessons brawn is the crave
Head of suspense, hand tight of money
Spoken words, voice as sweet as honey
Eyes wide shut for all knowledge isn't good
Learning ways of life as if turning hood
These situations caused a fence to be built
Mind caged in, gives the chance to wilt

Sweet Nothings

Kisses on the body begin to reveal
Anxious moments from your sex appeal
Playful fingers unleash a rub so soft
Critiques advances hoping they don't turn off
Push back hair while stroking the cheek
No beginning until reaching of top peak
Nibbling on the ear then ending in a bite
After all is said and done this will be an enjoyed flight
Still in the play of fore but ambitions are high
Not in the act of yet actions are spry
Thinking of diabetes from the sweetness of the neck
So the licks are timed and ended with a peck
New destination comes with exploring the navel
Pushing every button until no longer able
No hesitation taken while researching the thighs inner
Letting passion rise before indulging into dinner
At the risk of being called a tease
Sights are raised back to the nipples with ease

A Man

The earth moves as I sit still
Love to show strength at will
Reality strikes gently to raise a brow
Contemplating the time later or now
No pain notice the pricks from hair
Outbursts from sensitivity causes a stare
Expression of self worth fall on every page
Living life to know what gets better with age
Bathed in love and friends with grace
Near, far, in the perfect place
One's intuition could be a superstition
Pondering a future with little intermission
Spot a star then take aim
Believe in your dream in His name

Dreams

Withholding information from yourself is a crime
Strong information through codes of the mind
Few followers, but truth is given
Only thing on mind is completing the mission
Made false by a truth that was bigger
My only crime is being a nigger
The nightmare of all in my skin, my tone
Made into a criminal by one call of the phone
Left to die with peace at my side
Broke no laws, most I abide
No future will determine my movement
When it comes to this world it needs it needs improvement
Guided by glory, faith is there and sound
You are who you are when no one Is around
What is done in the dark will come to light
A soldier of colors in a losing fight
Bonds broken, truths withheld
My only future is a grave of jail
In the eyes of some racist cop
They decide on my future, I may succeed or flop
Afraid of the darkness, but allergic to the light
A decision to make, but either way it's a fight

Put It On Paper

I am not a vegetarian so I do not run from dead meat
I chase my main focus letting smoke relax me
I reply to the wrong fuck what you think
I see shots fired towards my eyes and did not blink
I smell smoke in the air so I search for its bearing
I am not a television so I can lack your starring
I belch out afterthoughts because they are better out than in
I thank God for not punishing me for every sin
I keep my baby sister closer than the nickname I gave
I walk by My Heart in life, even alone she is brave
I still remain clueless on how I arrived
I carry proof of each surgery I survived
I see the lie rising so I changed my view
I admit to lying at times more than few
I stand in front of the plaintiff and defendant
but missing a robe and gavel
I stay in clouds, but it is not by plane I travel
I exhale my reason after inhaling the lights green
I burn gas riding in an endless television screen
I hear portions of a story my seasons did not go
I failed to see resent episodes my mind is cluttered by dough
I overcome obstacles in more ways than one
I expressed surprise the next day when I was awaken by the sun
I know it is not my problem, but I am part of you both
I have not been married, but I know
for better or worse was in the oath
I saw a perfect family before I followed the streets
I wake up from my dream and continue
this nightmare every week
I anger my troubles by smiling over my pain

I search for sanity while a swisher sets flame
I hear no evil, those words flow to my left
I say I'm not a criminal, but if provoked I will still your breath
I look away from the eyes that have the truth far stretched
I throw money to no one, by me it is fetched
I daze deep off into an unexplored zone
I lay in bed at night thinking of a woman to call my own
I am not lost, I just do not know where I am
I if it does not concern money I do not give a damn
I let you know all of me just continue to read
I have room for one more in my life, my family is all I need

About The Author

Randy C. Young grew up in a seven person household in a trailer with two bedrooms and one bath. He shared a bed with his younger cousin and suffered with bladder issues that led to kidney failure.

Randy started writing poetry in the sixth grade at Notasulga High School. Being an older brother of two and sick led him to express himself through his poetry.

To contact the author, go to:
Email: randyyoung@yahoo.com
Facebook: Randy Young